The Meaning of Stars

RACHAEL LORD

Nymeria Publishing LLC

First published in the United States of America by Nymeria

Publishing LLC, 2023

Nymeria Publishing

PO Box 350747

Jacksonville, Fl 32235

Visit our website at www.nymeriapublishing.com

Print ISBN 979-8-9883332-2-7

1st Edition

Printed in U.S.A

For those who wish upon shooting stars.
May you find
what your heart desires.

For you.

Table of Contents

The Meaning of Stars

We are born of stardust
and heaven-sent kisses.
The conglomeration
of lives and love and legacies.

We trace the sky in every lifetime
as a promise,
a hope,
a belief,
a wish,
a dream.

And sometimes
we see ourselves in the glimmer:
our purpose,
our reason to be.

And often,
we are left wondering why the stars
won't twinkle the way
we want them to.

PART ONE
Constellations

My eyes never fail to find Orion.
Me, the center of his belt and you,
always there beside me.

You see, in the sky
it's black and white
a perfect alignment—
always you beside me.

The Stars Know My Secrets

The stars look much different
when you are five years old
and still believe they're full of magic.

Or when you're seven,
cradling a doll at the windowsill
wishing each night will be the one
he comes home.

When you're twelve,
screaming on the kitchen floor
because you are desperate
to be beyond them—
and it won't be the first time.

At thirteen,
when your friend looks back at you,
his face etched in the sky.

Or fifteen,
gazing up with your first love,
the starlight reflecting
in the naïveté of your eyes.

Twenty,
believing you are good enough
to be among them,
only to fall short
because you said so.

At twenty-four,

realizing that it might be enough
to simply be content
in the cosmic energy
and coordinates
that are meant for you.

Trying

The way you picked your head up
off the pillow
and took that first step today
when it felt
like you couldn't move
at all—
makes you fearless.

The way you put a smile
on the magnificence of your cheeks,
even if it was stolen
from someone else—
makes you a warrior.

The way you said I love you,
or hello
to a stranger—
it saved a life; I just know it.

The way we get through
is to try,
to pick ourselves up,
smile through the agony,
love without garnering anything in return.

And I want to assure you,
and perhaps myself,
that you,
that we,
are doing the very best we can.

Written in the Stars

You are made
of the same matter
as stardust.

Because of this
I crave to be reborn
in the sky

right beside you
in every lifetime

if I am so lucky.

The Preview of You

If I was presented
with a preview
of what our life
would be like,
all before I ever knew you,
I would've kept you
like a secret
and loved you
from our first

hello.

The Cycle of Life and Stars

From stars to dust
and back again
such as the cycle goes.

Our souls are sketched,
brilliantly new,
time and time again

running patterns
behind the clouds.

From One Poet to Another

I want to be
a great poet
but I don't think I know yet
how my words ebb
and flow much differently
than yours.

And I like to think
that's what makes everyone
a poet

because there is more
to the words
than simple rhyme or reason.

There is only truth
in the best way possible.

The Protagonist

We are all the main character,
the hero,
the protagonist
in the unfinished novel
of our singular existence.

But we are also the sidekick,
the comic relief,
the villain
in countless others.

Broken Beam

When you are broken
and smiling
it feels a lot like sun
shining
through the breaks
in the dark.

And it pokes through the clouds
to remind you
that once it shone
and once
it was beautiful.

We believe

that the last person out of bed
makes the bed.

We believe
in thrift store furniture
and dogs on the couch.

We believe
that Florida tap water
tastes like snot
and that happiness is more important
than money.

We believe
that stereos were meant to stay
at full volume
and that Black Lives Matter.

We believe
that education is a worthwhile
investment, and that love is love
is love is love.

We believe
in Monopoly game nights
and a women's right to choose.

We
believe
that people
and love
are worth believing in.

Shower me

with silent thoughts,
and twilight kisses

with promises,
broken or not,
with daydreams,
and melancholy purpose.

Shower me
with sunbeams
and rainwater,
the eternal kind of sunshine
that feels like the promise
of another day
with you.

Entangled Souls

I never needed anyone
until the moment
I first looked up
to see your eyes already on mine

and it was then
I knew
I was meant to love you

your soul permanently entangled
with mine.

Never Enough Time

I could love you
one hundred different ways
and it still wouldn't be
enough
when the time comes.

The Wrong One

When it aligns,
I beg you to wish on it.

And when it doesn't—
wish on it still.

Because the worst thing you could do
is spend your days
wondering if wishing on Ursa Major,
instead of turning your cheek
to Orion, to Lyra, to Sagittarius,
became the reason
you stopped believing in magic.

PART TWO

Shooting Stars

And sometimes
the fleeting flash of white light
in the dead of autumn
are wishes
set on a cosmic plan.

And sometimes
they are just airplanes.

The Light in the Dark

When it feels like
all the world is wrapped
in darkness
remember that you have
enough light
to shine through
the worst of it.

Walt Disney

taught me
to wish upon a shooting star
so that my true love
would come to save me.

But I think shooting stars
and Walt Disney
are full of shit
because I know
that I don't have to look
into someone else's eyes
to be saved.

A Day Away

Tomorrow
comes for you,
cries out for you,
begs you
to grab its hand
instead of mourn
its rise.

The Shine You Give

If a star
falls down
into your cupped hands—
it was meant for you
and only you to hold.

Don't give it away
to someone who will
bury it
in darkness.

Golden

I know the shimmer
of your golden heart
as solid as the god-like hands
that crafted it
worth more than love or fortune
or fame.

And I was the one
to find the fatal flaw
where no elegant, honey-glazed words
could ever explain away
why that heart of yours
beats for everyone
except you.

Cher

And sometimes
you see Cher
in a grocery store
and are too afraid
to get her autograph.

And sometimes
you let fear
sculpt you into the dumbest person
to ever live.

-based on a true story-

Moonshine

I'll tip my head back and
swallow the sting
of never again getting drunk on
moonbeams with you

not today,
not ever.

My Nightmares are a Disco Ball

The stars are shining
just for you
they used to shine
for me, too
but that was before they saw too much
of me
and shone the darkest parts for the world:
a disco ball of my
reckless being.

I am the queen

of selling myself short
but since I do not have
a crown
it does not count
as an accomplishment.

Control Freak

I am scared of things
I can't control
and not being around
to control them.

All that Remains

The birds sing their song to me, so
I close my eyes,
and listen to the garbling
that I know is heaven sent.

As soon as I realize,
it is only you, teasing me,
loving me
from the sky

I am content
at peace

I hope you are, too.

**My Letter to Teachers in the Midst of a Pandemic and
All the Times Before**

Jostle yourself alive
smell the lilac
and lavender
sprouts that have bloomed today
just for you.

They could not have
found their stems, or
blossomed
without your gentle spring,
your hand to guide them.

And I think that makes you
(even if you don't believe it)
pretty damn important.

Love is a Luxury Afforded to Poor Souls

There will always be
a part of me
that does not understand
how the human heart can go through so much
battering and bruising
only to come out
on the other side
ready to do it all over

again.

We're a lot alike, you and I

You like poetry,
sad things,
learning about World War Two

the color yellow
and when characters don't end up together

the word melancholy
and flopped Disney movies

songs about heartbreak,
even though you believe
in beautiful love,
and period dramas
and that's because a few

times, more than one hundred
we put ourselves into worlds
that make our nightmares seem
more or less blue.

And that's on empathy,
I think.

Therapy

looks like
writing poems
through hopeless tears

each one keeping me alive,
because the words make it so.

It's always yes or no

Yes,
everything will be okay
Yes,
this storm will pass
Yes,
my heart will find its way back to me
No,
I will not explain
why I grieve
this way
to you.

Growing Up, Up, and Away

Let all that you do
be lead with love
and let the words
that fall from your mouth
be anything but the hatred
you were taught to spout.

The Metaphor of Santa Claus

You were eight years old
once
and just starting
to understand logic

but you still believed
so fervently
in Santa Claus
though the pieces never quite fit together.

Like Mom
staying up late
on Christmas Eve
or the closed closet door
after November first.

But Santa was so real
and you had to believe
you just had to
because the thought of him being anything
but what your heart desired
was worse than not believing
at all.

-that's how you should believe in yourself-

Starry Eyed Optimist

Dreams are like flecks
of golden stardust
that rest on our temples
late at night
absorbing into the innocence
of our skin.

The speckled starfall tells us things
about ourselves that perhaps,
we already knew
or couldn't say out loud.

But when the specks of gold
land in our eye sockets midday,
as the sun kisses the sky

there's nothing we can do to stop
the bleary-eyed hope that comes
from visions of what may
or may not be.

Rise Up

Go ahead and rip
the skin from my bones,
steal my heart from
its casing.

Don't be afraid
to bludgeon my knees,
break my arms,
capture every one
of my breaths in a bottle.

Because even in pieces
I will rise

every single time.

It's a symphony, knowing who you are

And maybe,
just maybe,
the war inside my bones
will raise up
into an unfettered symphony

the likes of which
can be heard from the inside out.

The Broken Hearts Go Marching

When the broken hearts
fall into a dreamless sleep
that's when the flutters
of chest trapped butterflies
can dance happily

knowing that this moment of reprieve
feels like never being broken.

A glass doll

with bones of tapioca pudding,
though the stuff would never touch
her lips
for fear of being unloved.

All for Something

I don't need
heartfelt congratulations
but it does feel sweet
to know that my life's work,

the dream in my soul,
the patter of my heart was,
perhaps,
all for something.

I can count the people from my hometown

on both hands.
I could carry their ideology
in my back pocket.

There is a saying
made quite famous, that goes,
"There is no place like home."

It is where the heart is,
after all.

And I wonder
if I had let the pull
in my chest,
the longing of my heart,
lead me back
to that place—
would I be half the person I am today?

PART THREE

Making Stars out of Moon Rock

The chalked edges
on your fingertips
feel like happily ever after
and you hold it up to the sky
and you swear it twinkles
if you look hard enough.

Orion's Eyes

I spent my life
with my eyes to the sky:

I found Orion,
look at Orion.

Yet I could never be
as strong,
I could never
dream of being that noble
and bright.

But if I looked for long
enough,
I swore
I could see myself
in his starry
eyes.

The Astronomer

Astronomy
is a broken science

because
no amount of books
or evenings spent with an eye
to the telescope

can ever explain
why we're still
worlds apart.

Anomaly

If I was any farther
from perfect
I would be nestled
in a moon rock.

Or perhaps a star,
a black hole
a galaxy of pretty lies
and broken sheaths of promise.

Too many times
NASA has made their way to me,
and recoiled at the sight
of something so bright,
yet so incredibly odd.

In another life,

perhaps I wouldn't have had to try
so hard to win
your love

to win the
gleam
in your eyes.

Oxygen

I have loved you
for as long as I have breathed
and yet still
you hoard my breaths
like they are yours
and only yours
for the taking.

I never needed oxygen
the way I needed you.

I never needed to live
the way I cannot live
without you.

A Galaxy Not So Far Away

I live and exist as starlight
dancing
on the ceilings
of those who grew up
too damn fast

when the world was kind
until suddenly
it wasn't.

The Moon and its Fables

It was you,
me, and the moon

then I believed
it was only me

and finally,
it was just the moon.

Pennies in the Dark

Trying to find yourself
is tossing pennies
in the dark
and hoping a few turn up
the way they're supposed to.

What It's Like to be a Girl in 2010 or Anytime Across History

It's picked apart cuticles
and nervous foot taps

It's eat a cheeseburger
and "wow you've gained weight"

It's far too cheerful
and you should smile more

It's broken
and not shattered like them

It's beauty for the beholder
and too much makeup

It's too good
and never good enough.

The Cards Not Dealt

Life is a game of poker
and I am the player
who taps the table with anxious fingers,
betting my chips
in an all or nothing
kind of fashion.

Always the one
waiting patiently,
optimistically,
to see the combination
of life experiences
that can pile into the five cards
in my hands.

And then I am left wondering
always, always
wondering
what may have been
if the combination had been different.

Beauty in the Moon Rocks

The first man
on the moon
surely didn't realize
that he'd carry us back home
in his pocket

where we would forever
try to make stars
of ourselves.

Constantly told
that traveling
to distant galaxies
was better than holding
three hundred moon rocks.

So, we made ourselves
celestial and bright
without realizing that
there was so much
beauty in the broken pieces
of the moon.

PART FOUR

Blank, Starless Sky

When the sky is a canvas
of solid darkness,
and there isn't a twinkle
to be found,
it feels like maybe everything
was for nothing
and nothing
was the purpose
after all.

But they exist,
those stars,
behind a shadowed veil—

proof that they
were not meant for you
to see.

The Ghosts We Know

Achingly, I long for
all that we were
and what we could
have been.
Desperately clinging to
the things I imagined
about our great love story
that was cut short before
it even began.

I used to wear shorts
and a t-shirt
to play in the snow.

I was young then,
hurting then,
but I didn't know it.

Nowadays I bundle up
in 60 degrees
no doubt, because my heart
is icy now
my bones are frigid
shards of ice now.

I am the cold
now.

Candle in the Window

I am afraid
of candlelight
in which your eyes are lit
amidst the glow

because I know that one day
both will go out
and I won't know how
to light another candle.

Laurie

At seventeen,
you had my heart.
Loving you made it
hard to breathe,
but I ignored every sign and
inclination
that you felt differently.

I saw our
future, our
children, our
son
in the backyard, playing tag
with the neighbor's kids.

And I am here,
holding on to a belief
that I know won't save me
from the vacancy behind your stare.

I won't sit here and
beg you to love me,
but if I can persuade you
in the only way I know

then let me say
that I'm scared of a world
without you in it,
without the breathtaking view
of your face.

This is Not About Trains

The train skids to a stop
and the tracks briefly ignite
in a shower of electrical sparks.

The train contained only you—
my entire heart
sitting in the compartment
without so much as a single regret.

And you were such like the train that day
in that once you departed,
continued on your track,
you never bothered to take me with you
or come back to rescue me.

I shouted into the void for
every grueling moment
of the next few years,
but you never heard me
or came back to the station.

The Reality of Thought

"It's just a happy little daydream,"
she said,
as if her thoughts
were not already buried
six feet under
the earth.

Nothing

will ever feel sweeter
than the careful hurt
of loving you.

One day soon

I'll have to set you free
and I won't be ready
and it won't be easy
and I won't be able
to let you go.

In the West

Don't tell me
the sun sets for me
because I won't believe
that the sun could fall
just for me to see.

The Perfect Storm

I am the boat
and the sea,
the vessel
and its means
of destruction.

Unread

There is nothing more bizarre
and harrowing to the human experience
than realizing that after you die
you will continue to get emails.

Bath and Body Works
will still want us to know
that their hand soaps
are buy 3, get 2 free

and there will always be horny singles
in our respective areas.

The emails will collect
until Yahoo becomes irritated
and does absolutely nothing
about it.

And I guess what I'm trying
to say
is that even when we're gone
the world will still turn,
the emails will not stop,
and there is nothing
we can do
about any of it.

**Starlight,
star bright**

the devil is coming for me
tonight

I am reaching
for the first star I see.
I wish I may,
I wish I might.

Starlight,
Oh God,
star bright
there are only shadows
when there once was light.

The devil is calling, starlight
star bright

I can't see a thing

Hello darkness,
care to give a poor sinner some light?

Blind Faith

I used to believe
that everything
happened for a reason
until those reasons
bled into secrets
that weren't meant
for me to hear.

The lighthouse

beckons to me
from the rough waves
of never-ending nights.

It calls to me
through the light that passes
between my eyes
before returning to shadows
over and over and over again.

It is the hope of safe landing—
stillness,
and bare feet on the sand.

It yearns for me,
begs for my return.

And so,
I cannot understand
why I still turn my ship
in the other direction.

Bid me adieu,
kind light,
as you break against the dawn.
It was nice
to have you once
knowing well
that you will never shine
for me again.

I must thank you
for navigating
my path through the perfect storm
of everything I am.

But alas,
I must bid you adieu,
the light
that can no longer guide me
home.

PART FIVE

The Cosmos

"I don't belong here,"
　　you said,
　　when you were already
　　in your home
　　in the cosmos,

the place you were destined
　　to be
　　all along.

To the Girl Who Almost Didn't Make It

Oh, sweet girl,
look what you would have missed
if the storm had tucked you away
into its cloud.

Your first book
Your dream career
The love of your life
Your life.

Everything is for you, sweet girl
Every moment and breath
Every word I speak
Every stanza I write

And I hope you know
how proud I am
that you weathered the storm.

If all is fair in love and war,

then why does your smile
bring the armies
in my bones to
painstaking attention,
mistaking the flutter in my stomach
for a battle cry.

Social Anxiety

After any kind
of social gathering
I sit in my car
and think about
all the idiocies that may
or may not have spewed
from my mouth.

Most times,
I will have much to reflect
and punish myself for.

But when I did
everything right
and veiled my quirk to
perfection

I treat myself
to a silent round
of applause.

My body is a temple
or so you say—
tell me, wise man,
do you like my decorations?

My timid smile,
the terror in my eyes
as you walk close to me?

My favorite of these
is an ancient heirloom
passed down
from every woman before me

You see,
I put the keys
between my knuckles
just for you.

Queen of Broken Hearts

In the final cry of battle,
I hear the suckle sweet of your voice,
clinging and gnawing
at my ear drums.
I could savor it,
become lost in it, but I
don't.
I won't.

In the tattered wave of surrender,
I see that toothy grin,
a phantom drawl painted across
a frantic cloth,
which guts me from the inside out
to know that you're proud of me even so.

I was mistaken for a sinner
when I was always just afraid of the
girl in the looking glass.

I will always be the older sister

with attitude problems
and a grumpy demeanor
who keeps her sunshine
close to her chest
for fear of being misunderstood.

The ending of my youth

came as swiftly
as a fleshed-out nightmare. My twenties
over in a matter of seconds.

And I don't know that girl
that came
before

I don't recognize her
anymore.

Though she's nothing compared
to the resilient, fearsome
woman that rose
from the ashes.

The Great Lullaby

This one beautiful,
scary, delicate life
is ours to hold
in the pockets of our hearts,
in the whispers of a love song.

One beginning, middle, and end—
there are no wrong paths,
only unkept promises
and voyages not traveled.

Life, the great lullaby
that dips and crescendos in
a melody so beautiful
that even the final chord feels infinite.

It's beautiful, isn't it?
The melody of life?

So why am I so afraid
that I won't be able to hear it?

I worry too much

about things that are yet to be
or my inability to be
everywhere
and do everything
all at once.

I worry too much
about saying no
or disappointing someone I admire, always
talking myself out of a daydream.

I worry too much
about breaking someone's heart
or what they must think of me
now that I've completely ruined their day.

I worry too much
about sprinting hard and fast,
overworking, overthinking

and I never stop to think
why my heart is so far behind,
unable to catch up.

Swimsuit Season

Summer weeds stand, stubborn
like "too thick" arm hairs
and stubbled pits, backs, and bellies,
forgotten under sleeves
and jeans.

The humidity settles
as a warning: don't you dare go outside
in that outfit.

I hear the seagulls
squawking, mocking my fear
as my toes sink into sand
and I wrap myself tight in
a pretty towel.

It's the onset of summer
which can only mean two things:
1) I am afraid of
2) swimsuit season.

But as my towel
turns to dust on the shoreline
I am reminded that
3) we are all worthy of a joyful existence
and 4) we were not put on this Earth for critique
because 5) there is perfection, beauty in the way we exist
alone, meaning that
6) every body is a swimsuit body.

-I dare you to wear that outfit-

Aftermath

You thought you'd take
my power
but honey,
I'm the villain now.

Master of Disguise

You learn to live
the life created for you

You learn to get by
in the mistakes
you didn't mean to make

You learn that who you were
and are
are two very different bodies
entirely

You learn that your body
is yours and yours
alone

And you know what?
You learn to love it all, too.

Mosaic

I am a brilliant mosaic
of all the people
I have even known.

I've collected each piece
that I like best:
their hearts,
the sounds of their laughter
the way they go about life
like nobody is watching

and I pieced them together
to create the version of me that
I most admire.

And it is my hope
that someone will think me
worthy enough
to take a piece from who I've created

-a legacy of human experience-

Picasso and Me

To love
is to paint yourself
on a canvas
and hope that someone
likes the abstract nature
of your art.

Legacy

When the sky
is a brilliant hue
of sapphire
as rare as the face
that gazes upon it,
star lit and upturned,
a smile that holds
the galaxy of your legacy

that is when life
begins to make sense.

-loving someone-

Whispers All the Time

I could be happy too,
if the voices
quieted.

The Sun is a Star

I can taste its beauty
on the tip of my tongue
sometimes
I can touch its fire
with my fingertips
most days
I can feel it's breath-like warmth
on my skin
when I feel most alive in it

I can feel it all around me
like a sun-soaked kiss
but when it isn't beautiful
and it isn't bright
and it's tucked behind a cloud
I can only touch and taste and feel
the ice and the dark...

and God, I'm shivering.

The Last Door on the Left

You force a handle
on a door
that won't budge,
desperation clawing at your throat
as you sink against the frame,
your knuckles sore from
the trauma.

You believe with your entire soul
that you have fallen short
of your destiny because without
one foot
through that threshold,
what is your worth, anyway?

But doors weren't meant to be pried open
and you were not meant to sulk outside
like a shadow awaiting eternity.

See, doors only open if there's a life
behind them
and maybe it's the next one
or the next, or the one down the hall
where the lock will finally click

and not a moment sooner.

Young enough

to be stupid enough
to dream enough wild things
to circle the Earth
more than enough times.

And yet, I like to think
that I am worthy enough,
even smart enough,
to know that I am enough.

Vodka Sunrise

Every day is a battle
of my own dilution:
do I talk less and
bite my tongue today?

Do I laugh out loud or
chuckle softly,
a tepid girl,
a more palatable representation?

Should I be the vodka sunrise
I was always meant to be
or will I simply amount to
watered down OJ
in a glass half empty?

If I break myself open,
expose too much of who I am,
will you still want to know me?

If your answer is no,
then I'll be content to drink alone.

-vodka sunrise it is-

Dance Until Death and Dawn

The universe
will make a mockery
of you

but in the dance
of this crazy, merciless
life you will make
a mockery of it, too.

-dance until your heart stops beating-

In Memory Of

the girl I once knew
and loved.

The truth is
I don't know who I am
anymore.

So, here's to mourning
what could've been
had I stayed the same girl my whole life.

The stars betrayed me.

I'd like to tip my chin and scream
from the bottom of my soul,
but I know they'd only cackle back
and whisper:
this was always meant to happen to you.

I did everything right
I was a vessel
of perfect cosmic energy

but the night the stars betrayed me
the shine burned a hole in my heart.

Black holes don't suck

and constellations are just
coincidence.

Stars don't twinkle
and the sun is just another one of them.

Yet on the stars
we wish and pray and hope
that we'll find our way

but really
it was us
the
whole
damn
time.

Acknowledgments

I thought about starting this collection with a foreword that would explain this collection and its intentions, the "why" of it all. But then I thought, what a better way to acknowledge the journey of this collection than through, you guessed it, the acknowledgements.

When I started writing this collection in late 2020, I set out to write poems that analyzed the stars, the constellations, the meanings behind common phrases, especially the notion that "everything is written in the stars."

I used to believe that phrase wholeheartedly. Keyword: used.

I wrote the first draft of this collection rather quickly. And then, a life experience plummeted me into a horrific depression and suddenly this collection took on a whole new meaning. Through multiple rounds of editing, I found a new meaning within these words. A meaning I didn't ask for.

Where do you turn when the stars have forsaken you?

What happens when there are no stars left to guide you?

Is there a way to find meaning in them at all?

This collection is my attempt at answering those questions, to make sense of the chaos in my mind. Perhaps, that makes me a cynic. I would argue that I've been forced to look at things as they really are, not what I wish they could become. No matter how much I begged or pleaded or desired for things to work or make sense. If you would have asked me what the meaning of the stars was back in 2020, I would have told you that the stars are there to guide you.

What's the meaning of the stars to me now?

It's me. It's you.

That's it.

Now on to the amazing people that made this collection possible.

This collection wouldn't exist without Kennedy and Sarah at Nymeria Publishing who believed in yet another one of my poetry collections. Your guidance, editorial advice, and friendship all mean the absolute world to me. I am so lucky to know you both. Thank you endlessly.

To those who helped me find my way through some of the darkness moments of my life, thank you. You know who you are. This book is for you.

Thank you to Maddie Zahm, whose music fueled the rewrites and editing process for this collection. Your music speaks to my soul. Your songs speak to this collection in so many ways.

And to you— the wonderful human reading this book— thank you, thank you, thank you. I hope you find your own version of the stars. But mostly, I hope you never forget how magical

and special you are.

xoxo,

Rachael